The Summer of Black Widows

Books by Sherman Alexie

Poetry:

The Business of Fancydancing
First Indian on the Moon
Old Shirts & New Skins

Fiction:

The Lone Ranger and Tonto Fistfight in Heaven
Reservation Blues
Indian Killer

Limited Editions:

I Would Steal Horses
Seven Mourning Songs for the Cedar Flute I Have Yet to Learn to Play
Water Flowing Home

SHERMAN ALEXIE

The Summer of Black Widows

Hanging Loose Press
Brooklyn, New York

Published by Hanging Loose Press, 231 Wyckoff Street, Brooklyn, New York 11217.

Printed in the United States of America
10 9 8 7 6 5

Acknowledgments

Some of these poems have been published in the following magazines and anthologies: *Aboriginal Voices, Alternative Press, Beloit Poetry Journal, The Best American Poetry 1996, Caliban, Chiron Review, College English, Forkroads, Free Lunch, Graffiti Rag, Hanging Loose, Impetus, Indiana Review, Journal of All Thought, The Ledge, Many Mountains Moving, Pacific Northwest Inlander, Pemmican, Ploughshares, Prairie Schooner, Rain City Review, Red Brick Review, Seattle Weekly, Semi-Dwarf Quarterly, Urbanus,* and *ZYZZYVA.*

And some of these poems have been published in *Water Flowing Home,* a Limberlost Press limited-edition chapbook.

The author wishes to thank the Lila Wallace-Reader's Digest Writers' Awards for their support during the writing of some of these poems.

Hanging Loose Press wishes to thank the Literature Programs of the National Endowment for the Arts and the New York State Council on the Arts for grants in support of this book's publication.

Cover art by Melissa Zexter
Cover design by Caroline Drabik

Library of Congress Cataloging-in-Publication Data

Alexie, Sherman
The summer of black widows / Sherman Alexie
p. cm.
ISBN 1-882413-35-0. — ISBN 1-882413-34-2 (pbk.)
I. Title.
PS3551.L35774S86 1996 96-9822
818'.5409—dc20 CIP

Contents

Why We Play Basketball

After the First Lightning 11
The Summer of Black Widows 12
Defending Walt Whitman 14
Mistranslation of a Traditional Spokane Indian Song 16
Glossary of a Powwow 17
The First and Last Ghost Dance of Lester FallsApart 18
That Place Where Ghosts of Salmon Jump 19
Song of Ourself 20
Why We Play Basketball 21

Father and Farther

Haibun 29
Grandmother, Porcupine, Traffic 31
Totem Sonnets 32
When I Was My Father I Sang Love Songs to My Son 39
Father and Farther 40
Diabetes 44
Death of the Landlord 45

Sister Fire, Brother Smoke

Elegies 49
Fire as Verb and Noun 52
Sonnet: Tattoo Tears 56
Sister Fire, Brother Smoke 60

Grand Entry

The Lover of Maps 63
How We Learn to Say "Mouth" and "Hand" and "Small of Back" 64
Marriage 65
Grand Entry 66
Drum as Love, Fear, and Prayer 68
Last Will and Testament 73

Tourists

Harmful Jazz ... 77
Owl Dancing with Fred Astaire ... 78
Airplane ... 81
Prayer Animals ... 84
How to Remodel the Interior of a Catholic Church ... 85
Capital Punishment ... 86
Tourists ... 91
How to Write the Great American Indian Novel ... 94
The Exaggeration of Despair ... 96
The Powwow at the End of the World ... 98
What We Notice, What We Miss ... 99

To Find Sasquatch

The Sasquatch Poems ... 103

Bob's Coney Island

Introduction to Western Civilization ... 113
After the Trial of Hamlet, Chicago, 1994 ... 114
Inside Dachau ... 117
Reading Harvey Shapiro's Poetry While Standing in Line to See Tom Hanks in *Apollo 13* ... 123
Things (for an Indian) to do in New York (City) ... 124
Going to the Movies with Geronimo's Wife ... 131
The Museum of Tolerance ... 133
Airplane, Airport, Airline, Air in the Bottom of the Ninth Inning ... 134
Bob's Coney Island ... 138

for Diane

Why We Play Basketball

After the First Lightning

I will ask your permission
to weave a story
from your hair, weave it

around both of us
as we sit, warm and safe
on the hill above
the reservation and all

her skins, watch
the first storm of the year
approach, pass over
then move away.

The Summer of Black Widows

The spiders appeared suddenly
after that summer rainstorm.

Some people still insist the spiders fell with the rain
while others believe the spiders grew from the damp soil like weeds
with eight thin roots.

The elders knew the spiders
carried stories in their stomachs.

We tucked our pants into our boots when we walked through fields
of fallow stories.
An Indian girl opened the closet door and a story fell into her hair.
We lived in the shadow of a story trapped in the ceiling lamp.
The husk of a story museumed on the windowsill.
Before sleep, we shook our blankets and stories fell to the floor.
A story floated in a glass of water left on the kitchen table.
We opened doors slowly and listened for stories.
The stories rose on hind legs and offered their red bellies to the most
beautiful Indians.
Stories in our cereal boxes.
Stories in our firewood.
Stories in the pockets of our coats.
We captured stories and offered them to the ants, who carried the
stories back to their queen.
A dozen stories per acre.
We poisoned the stories and gathered their remains with broom and
pan.

The spiders disappeared suddenly
after that summer lightning storm.

Some people still insist the spiders were burned to ash

while others believe the spiders climbed the lightning bolts and
became a new constellation.

The elders knew the spiders
had left behind bundles of stories.

Up in the corners of our old houses
we still find those small, white bundles
and nothing, neither fire
nor water, neither rock nor wind,
can bring them down.

Defending Walt Whitman

Basketball is like this for young Indian boys, all arms and legs
and serious stomach muscles. Every body is brown!
These are the twentieth-century warriors who will never kill,
although a few sat quietly in the deserts of Kuwait,
waiting for orders to do something, do something.

God, there is nothing as beautiful as a jump shot
on a reservation summer basketball court
where the ball is moist with sweat
and makes a sound when it swishes through the net
that causes Walt Whitman to weep because it is so perfect.

There are veterans of foreign wars here,
whose bodies are still dominated
by collarbones and knees, whose bodies still respond
in the ways that bodies are supposed to respond when we are young.
Every body is brown! Look there, that boy can run
up and down this court forever. He can leap for a rebound
with his back arched like a salmon, all meat and bone
synchronized, magnetic, as if the court were a river,
as if the rim were a dam, as if the air were a ladder
leading the Indian boy toward home.

Some of the Indian boys still wear their military haircuts
while a few have let their hair grow back.
It will never be the same as it was before!
One Indian boy has never cut his hair, not once, and he braids it
into wild patterns that do not measure anything.
He is just a boy with too much time on his hands.
Look at him. He wants to play this game in bare feet.

God, the sun is so bright! There is no place like this.
Walt Whitman stretches his calf muscles
on the sidelines. He has the next game.

His huge beard is ridiculous on the reservation.
Some body throws a crazy pass and Walt Whitman catches it with
quick hands.
He brings the ball close to his nose
and breathes in all of its smells: leather, brown skin, sweat, black hair,
burning oil, twisted ankle, long drink of warm water,
gunpowder, pine tree. Walt Whitman squeezes the ball tightly.
He wants to run. He hardly has the patience to wait for his turn.
"What's the score?" he asks. He asks, "What's the score?"

Basketball is like this for Walt Whitman. He watches these Indian boys
as if they were the last bodies on earth. Every body is brown!
Walt Whitman shakes because he believes in God.
Walt Whitman dreams of the Indian boy who will defend him,
trapping him in the corner, all flailing arms and legs
and legendary stomach muscles. Walt Whitman shakes
because he believes in God. Walt Whitman dreams
of the first jump shot he will take, the ball arcing clumsily
from his fingers, striking the rim so hard that it sparks.
Walt Whitman shakes because he believes in God.
Walt Whitman closes his eyes. He is a small man and his beard
is ludicrous on the reservation, absolutely insane.
His beard makes the Indian boys laugh righteously. His
beard frightens
the smallest Indian boys. His beard tickles the skin
of the Indian boys who dribble past him. His beard, his beard!

God, there is beauty in every body. Walt Whitman stands
at center court while the Indian boys run from basket to basket.
Walt Whitman cannot tell the difference between
offense and defense. He does not care if he touches the ball.
Half of the Indian boys wear T-shirts damp with sweat
and the other half are bareback, skin slick and shiny.
There is no place like this. Walt Whitman smiles.
Walt Whitman shakes. This game belongs to him.

Mistranslation of a Traditional Spokane Indian Song

and then bear says to me
that he wishes he did not have to sleep through winter
because he has seen the photograph
and is quite convinced
that snow is most beautiful
on the midnight basketball court
of a reservation town
where the dark ghosts of Indian children
leave no trace of their passing
as they run from hoop to hoop
way ya hi yo
way ya hi yo

Glossary of a Powwow

women's traditional dancer

her beads
affect the weather

men's traditional dancer

his feathers
will not fall

jingle dress dancer

she creates more music
than a symphony

grass dancer

he sways within
his own storm

fancy shawl dancer

she wears wings
outside the aviary

men's fancydancer

he mimics
his favorite color

children

this is not practice
they are dancing

The First and Last Ghost Dance of Lester FallsApart

It rained buffalo
in a wheat field
just off the reservation.

Confused and homeless
but otherwise free
of injury, the buffalo were rounded up and shipped
to Spokane's Walk in the Wild Zoo.

From behind a symbolic chain link fence
the buffalo stared
                                        intelligently

at white visitors
who soon became very nervous.

Everything beautiful
begins somewhere.

That Place Where Ghosts of Salmon Jump

Coyote was alone and angry because he could not find love.
Coyote was alone and angry because he demanded a wife

from the Spokane, the Coeur d'Alene, the Palouse, all those tribes
camped on the edge of the Spokane River, and received only laughter.

So Coyote rose up with his powerful and senseless magic
and smashed a paw across the water, which broke the river bottom

in two, which created rain that lasted for forty days and nights,
which created Spokane Falls, that place where salmon travelled

more suddenly than Coyote imagined, that place where salmon swam
larger than any white man dreamed. Coyote, I know you broke

the river because of love, and pretended it was all done by your design.
Coyote, you're a liar and I don't trust you. I never have

but I do trust all the stories the grandmothers told me.
They said the Falls were built because of your unrequited love

and I can understand that rage, Coyote. We can all understand
but look at the Falls now and tell me what you see. Look

at the Falls now, if you can see beyond all of the concrete
the white man has built here. Look at all of this

and tell me that concrete ever equals love. Coyote,
these white men sometimes forget to love their own mothers

so how could they love this river which gave birth
to a thousand lifetimes of salmon? How could they love

these Falls, which have fallen farther, which sit dry
and quiet as a graveyard now? These Falls are that place

where ghosts of salmon jump, where ghosts of women mourn
their children who will never find their way back home,

where I stand now and search for any kind of love,
where I sing softly, under my breath, alone and angry.

Song of Ourself

While Walt Whitman sang about his body, the still body of one Indian grew into two, then ten, then multitudes.

Why We Play Basketball

1.

In December, snow
covered the court. We
wrapped our hands in old
socks, soaked the white snow
with kerosene, lit

the match, and melted it
all down to pavement.
We were Indians
who wanted to play
basketball. Nothing

could stop us from that,
not the hunger in
our thin bellies, not
the fear of missed shots,
not the threat of white

snow. We were small boys
who would grow into
small men. We played ball
until dark, then played
until we could see

neither hoop nor ball.
We played until our
mothers and fathers
came searching for us
and carried us home.

2.

We play because we
remember the first
time we shot the ball
and knew, beyond doubt,
as it floated toward

the hoop, that it was
going to be good.
We walked off the court,
left the ball waiting
as we fell in love

with Indian girls
who grew past us, who
grew into Indian
women. Somehow, we
grew families while

that ball waited, in-
ert, suspended, till
we remembered, with
a complex rush of
pain and joy, what we'd

left behind, how we
loved the ball as it
finally dropped in-
to the net, after
years of such patience.

3.

We wanted to know
who was best, who could
change the game into
something new. We knew
about Seymour. Blind

and deaf, he played by
sense of smell. Leather
balls drove him crazy.
He identified
his teammates by tribe:

Spokanes smelled like bread;
Flatheads smelled like pine;
Colville smelled like snow;
Lester smelled like wine.
Seymour shot the ball

when the wind told him
it was time to shoot.
In basketball, we
find enough reasons
to believe in God,

or something smaller
than God. We believe
in Seymour, who holds
the ball in his hands
like you hold your God.

4.

It is just a game
we are told by those
who cannot play it
unless it is play.
For us, it is war,

often desperate
and without reason.
We throw our body
against another
body. We learn to

hate each other, hate
the ball, hate the hoop,
hate the fallen snow,
hate our clumsy hands,
hate our thirsty mouths

when we drink from
the fountain. We hate
our fathers. We hate
our mothers. We hate
the face in our mirror.

We play basketball
because we want to
separate love from
hate, and because we
know how to keep score.

5.

We play basketball
because we still love
the place where we lived.
It was a small house
with one door. We lived

there for twenty years
with crazy cousins
and one basketball.
We fought over it
constantly. I climbed

into a tall tree
with the ball, refused
to come down unless
they made me captain.
My brother dragged me

from the tree and punched
me so hard I saw
red horses. We play
because we believe
in our skins and hands.

These hands hold the ball.
These hands hold the tribe.
These hands build fires.
We are a small tribe.
We build small fires.

Father and Farther

Haibun

In the spring of 1954, two non-Indian brothers, James and John, and a Chippewa named Leo, went searching for God on the Spokane Indian Reservation. It was midnight. They carried Geiger counters and a mineral light. They found pieces of God whispering beneath a spur of Lookout Mountain. When they cracked open the earth, it was so bright that it fooled the birds, who lifted into flight.

> The half-life of a raven
> is still a life.
> Raven stopped the Flood.

First came the arguments about claim rights. Then came the mining companies and the government. In 1956, they paid $340,000 for the land that bordered the claim. My cousins Richard and Lucy Boyd, brother and sister, received most of the money. Lucy died in a car wreck in 1961. In 1969, Richard choked to death on a piece of steak. They buried both on the reservation, though I have never visited their graves.

> A rusty tin cup
> sits on a woodstove
> in the abandoned house.

The uranium trucks rolled for most of two decades, dropping hot dust on the heads of Indian children standing beside the road. I remember waving to the truck drivers, who were all white men. I remember they always waved back. When the mines closed down, the empty trucks rumbled away. I cannot tell you how many coffins we filled during the time of the trucks, but we learned to say "cancer" like we said "oxygen" and "love."

> Grandmother died on her couch
> covered with seven quilts,
> one for each of her children.

The white men quickly abandoned the mine. They left behind pools of dirty water, barrels of dirty tools, and mounds of dirty landfill. They taught us that "dirty" meant "safe." After the white men left, Indians guarded the mine. My uncle worked the graveyard shift. If he listened closely as he made his rounds, he could hear Chimakum Creek, just a few hundred feet to the south.

In this light
we can see the bones of salmon
as they swim.

For decades, we Spokanes stared into the bright sky with envy and built flimsy wings for ourselves. For decades, we pressed our breasts and scrotums in a new kind of ceremony. Now, in 1994, the white men have come back to clean what they left behind. They plan to dig deeper holes and fill them with fresh water. They plan to dump indigenous waste into those lakes, and then add waste shipped in from all over the country. They gave us a 562-page bible that explains why we cannot stop them.

Two suns:
Abel fell from the sky,
Cain rose from the lake.

Grandmother, Porcupine, Traffic

When Big Mom saw porcupine
dead in the middle of any road
she ordered the car stopped.

Big Mom stopped
traffic as she stepped in the road
and dragged the old porcupine

from the pavement. The crushed porcupine
thick with quills, but that never stopped
Big Mom. Beside the road

she pulled quills from its skin. The road
filled with slowed cars. The porcupine
full of blood, stopped

and cold. Big Mom never stopped
long enough to notice the road
had ceased to be road. The porcupine

would always be porcupine
no matter that its heart had stopped.
Its sharp quills were more useful than a road.

I never stepped in the road
with Big Mom and porcupine.
To this day, I have neither stopped

nor slowed my life, never stopped
to pull porcupine from the road
because I loved porcupine.

Big Mom loved porcupine
even as she grew too old to have the car stopped
and cried as she left porcupine alone on the road.

Totem Sonnets

1

Meryl Streep
Emily Dickinson
Dian Fossey
Flannery O'Connor
John Steinbeck
Helen Keller
Walt Whitman
Bruce Springsteen

Kareem Abdul-Jabbar
Zora Neale Hurston
Frida Kahlo
Pablo Neruda
Harriet Tubman
Muhammad Ali

2

Steamed Rice
Whole Wheat Bagel
Egg White
Baked Chicken

Tomato Soup
Broccoli
Cheddar Cheese
Garlic Clove

Grape Nuts and Non-Fat Milk
Almonds
Apple
Ice Water

Insulin
Hypodermic

3

Crazy Horse
Sitting Bull
Captain Jack
Black Kettle
Ishi
Joseph
Qualchan
Wovoka

Anna Mae Aquash
Wilma Mankiller
Tantoo Cardinal
Winona LaDuke
Buffy Sainte-Marie
Maria Tallchief

4

The Exorcist
Manhunter
Alien
Halloween

Star Wars
Escape from New York
Silent Running
Terminator

Little Big Man
Enter the Dragon
The Searchers
The Wild Bunch

Midnight Cowboy
The Graduate

5

Buddy Holly
Joni Mitchell
The Beatles
Janis Joplin
Hank Williams
Patsy Cline
The Ramones
Lou Reed

Robert Johnson
Sippie Wallace
Charley Patton
Memphis Minnie
Jaybird Coleman
Muddy Waters

6

Lenny
Edgar Bearchild
Holden Caulfield
Tess

The Misfit
Sula
Mazie
Tayo

Cacciato
Cecelia Capture
Hamlet
Jim Loney

Daredevil
The Incredible Hulk

7

Jesus Christ
Adam
Mary Magdalene
Eve

Jim Thorpe
Billy Mills
Billie Jean King
Ann Meyers

John Lennon
D.B. Cooper
Amelia Earhart
Martin Luther King, Jr.

Mother
Father

When I Was My Father I Sang Love Songs to My Son

Drunk like that, I
imagined myself as

you, drunk like that
and carried the same

small ambition: I
only wanted to live

one day longer than you.

Father and Farther

Such waltzing was not easy.
—Theodore Roethke

1.

In McNeil Island Prison for bad checks, my father worked to pay back his debts. One morning, a few weeks before his scheduled release date, he climbed the power tower for some routine line repair and touched a live wire. Unconscious and burned, he fell five feet before his safety line snapped taut.

2.

My father knows how to jitterbug.
How many Indians can say that?

3.

He attended Catholic school on purpose. There, the nuns taught him how to play piano. He refuses to play now, and offers no explanations for his refusal. There is a photograph of my father and his sister sitting side by side at a piano. She is wearing a silk dress. He is wearing a coat and tie. Did she know how to play the piano? I assume she could. She attended the same Catholic school as my father. She died in 1980. My father stood beside her coffin and did not sing.

4.

Late night, Yakama Indian Reservation, my father drunk, telling stories. We had traveled there to play in an all-Indian basketball tournament. My father was the coach. I was the shooting guard. We had a bad team and were eliminated quickly. We camped in a cheap hotel. Four players to a room, though my father and I were alone for some reason. "Listen," my father said, "I was a paratrooper in the war." "Which war?" I asked. "All of them," he said.

5.

My father drinks cough syrup
because he believes it heals everything.

My father drinks cough syrup
because he watched RFK's last news conference.

My father drinks cough syrup
because he has a tickle in the back of his throat.

My father drinks cough syrup
because he has survived twenty-three car wrecks.

My father drinks cough syrup
because he wants to stop the influenza virus at the door.

My father drinks cough syrup
because he once saw Lana Turner in a parade.

My father drinks cough syrup
because he is afraid of medicine.

6.

Of course, by now, you realize this is a poem about my father. It could also be a series of exaggerations and outright lies. I might be talking about another man who wears my father's mask. Behind that mask, he could be anybody.

7.

Summer evening, 1976. Our father is thirsty. He knows his children are thirsty. He rummages through our house in search of loose change. He finds a handful of coins. He walks to the Spokane Tribal Jail which, for some unknown reason, has the only soda pop machine on the reservation. My father has enough change for six Pepsis. It is quiet. We can hear mosquitoes slamming against the screen door. The jail is only a few hundred feet from our house. If we listen closely, we can hear our father dropping change into the machine. We can hear the sodas drop into the dispenser. My father gathers the cans. He carries them back to us.

8.

Basketball is
a series of prayers.

Shoot the ball
and tell me

you believe
otherwise.

My father
shoots the ball.

As it spins away
my father prays.

9.

My father often climbed into a van with our crazy cousins and left us for days to drink. When he came back, still drunk, he always popped "Deer Hunter" into the VCR. He never made it past the wedding scene. I kept watching it after he'd passed out. Halfway through the movie, John Savage and Robert De Niro play a sick game of Russian Roulette while their Vietcong captors make wagers on the probable survivor. De Niro asks for more bullets. Two bullets, three. He knows the odds. He holds the gun to his head. He has a plan.

10.

As he dribbles
past you, into the
paint, then stops, pivots
and gives the big man
a head fake, you must
remember that my
father can shoot with either
the right or left hand.

11.

During the World's Fair in 1974, my father and I rode over Spokane Falls in a blue gondola. No. It was more like a chair. Our legs and feet floated free. I looked down into the water. My father held his left arm around me. He must have been afraid of gravity. Then my left shoe came loose because the laces were not tight enough. My shoe would have slipped from my foot if I hadn't pressed my other shoe against it. My father told me to hang on. He was smiling as I struggled to keep my shoe. I had written my name across the top of it. I looked down into the water. My father was laughing. The chair was blue. It was 1974. The entire world was walking the streets below us. My mother was dancing for tourists in the Native American exhibit. My siblings were sleeping in the station wagon. Gravity. The water. My shoe. I looked at my father. He held me tightly. He told me to hold on.

Diabetes

Having learned sugar kills me
piece by piece, I have to eat
with more sense
than taste

so I travel alone in this
limited feast, choosing
the right place
and plate

and take the hard bread exactly
in my teeth, knowing what
the bread contains is
what contains me.

Death of the Landlord

My landlord died.
His wife sits alone

in her kitchen
across the street.

I can see her
through the window.

This is not about my father.

He was a good landlord.
He hired men from halfway houses

to mow the lawn.
My landlord trusted

they would not steal.
He offered them water.

This is not about my father.

The landlord's wife mourns.
She holds a clean cup.

She gathered my mail
when I was away

and kept it behind a chair
in her living room.

The door was unlocked.
I'd enter quietly

and take my mail
without disturbing their sleep.

My landlord slept
in an oxygen tent.

My landlord's wife falls
asleep in her favorite chair.

This is not about my father.

My landlord stood
on his front porch

and waved to me
as my taxi left

for the airport.
I always promised

to stop and visit
when I returned

with news of my world.
My landlord has left

all of our worlds.
His wife drives away

in a blue car
to her grandson's wedding.

She waves.
I wave back.

I am leaving myself soon
to live in a different city.

This is not about my father.

When mourning
I stand still.

When mourning
I hold my breath.

When mourning
I stand still.

When mourning
I exhale.

This is not about my father.

Sister Fire, Brother Smoke

Elegies

This is a poem for people who died in stupid ways.
This is a poem for Napoleon's great-grandson who snapped his neck when his ridiculously long scarf caught in the rear wheels of the convertible he was driving.
This is a poem for General George Armstrong Custer.
This is a poem for all the Japanese gourmets who eat one of those poisonous blowfish, which are considered a great delicacy, but are lethal in even the smallest portions unless prepared expertly by a chef who has trained for years. A blowfish steak will make your lips numb, blur your vision, and ring your ears, when it is prepared correctly. A poorly prepared blowfish will stop your heart just like that. The dead, with their stuffed, stopped hearts, are buried with expressions of deep satisfaction.
This is a poem for all those who died with expressions of deep satisfaction.
This is a poem for the skydivers who pulled the cord and heard the deafening silence of a chute that would not open, then felt the roar of the secondary chute as it fluttered uselessly above them.
This is a poem for all of the teenagers who tried to beat the train at the crossing and failed.
This is a poem for all of the folksingers who wrote songs about teens who have failed to beat the train at the crossing.
This is a poem for the Brink's armored-car guard who was crushed to death by $50,000 worth of quarters. He was guarding a load of twenty-five-pound coin boxes in the back of a truck when the driver braked suddenly to avoid a car that had swerved in front of him. When the driver pulled over to check on his partner, he found him completely covered by coins.
This is a poem for all the hunger strikers of the world. When they are close to death, I forget why they were striking. I just want to give them a glass of water and a slice of bread. After they are gone, I feel motion sickness.
This is a poem for the men and women who ate themselves to death

with meals of such enormity (whole chickens, ten pounds of eggs, gallons of milk, twenty-seven apple pies) that their hearts simply collapsed.

This is a poem for the cooks who prepared those enormous meals and feel no guilt.

This is a poem for the cooks who prepared those enormous meals and feel guilty.

This is a poem for smokers.

This is a poem for the poet who camped on Mount St. Helen's just days before the mountain erupted, despite repeated warnings from experts and psychics alike.

This is a poem for anybody who camps on active volcanoes. I am the kind of man who makes rules for himself. Hence, I forbid myself to become the kind of man who camps on active volcanoes. Please feel free to adopt this rule for yourself.

This is a poem for the people who jump off the Golden Gate Bridge and change their minds halfway down.

This is a poem for everybody who jumps off the Golden Gate Bridge because they all change their minds halfway down. I have faith that nobody wants to die for any time period longer than the few seconds it actually takes to commit suicide.

This is a poem for the music student who died after being caught in a flash fire while trying to relieve a bad case of hemorrhoids with gasoline. Don't ask me about the details.

This is a poem for John Edward Blue, who was being baptized on August 13, 1984, when he and the minister performing the baptism slipped and fell backward into deep water. The minister survived, but Blue drowned.

This is a poem for the minister who survived. He sits alone now and prays quietly for clarity and forgiveness.

This is a poem for me. No. This is a poem for the me I used to be, the me who once drove drunk on purpose, knowing I was too drunk to drive well, quite sure I might die in a crash. I was the me who changed his mind halfway through the ride, stopped the car in the middle of the road, and walked home. The car was still running, engine idling, when the tow truck arrived a few hours later.

This is a poem for the me who kept driving and crashed through a guardrail into the river, or smashed head-on into a car full of teenagers returning from a high school basketball game, or rolled over twenty-two times, down the highway, car coming to a rest on its wheels, roof collapsed on my head.

This is a poem for my oldest brother, who is still alive and living with our parents on the reservation, but who I worry about when my telephone rings in Seattle. Every so often, I have to catch my breath before I can pick up the receiver.

This is a poem for my oldest sister and her husband, who died in a trailer fire in Montana when a curtain drifted on wind and touched a hot plate left burning. My sister and her husband were passed out in the back bedroom, too drunk to wake, even when the flames and smoke danced through their bedroom.

This is a poem for my father, who has a sore on his foot that will never heal. He salts his food with vengeance, like he was taking revenge on everybody who had ever done him wrong.

This is a poem for my tribe, who continue to live in the shadow of the abandoned uranium mine on our reservation, where the night sky glows in a way that would have invoked songs and stories a few generations earlier, but now simply allows us to see better as we drive down the highway toward a different kind of moon.

Fire as Verb and Noun

> *Working from a carefully developed understanding of his place in an oppressed culture, [Alexie] focuses on the need to tear down obstacles before nature tears them down. Fire is therefore a central metaphor: a sister and brother-in-law killed, a burnt hand, cars aflame.*
> —Publisher's Weekly

> *Sherman, I'm so sorry your sister was killed by a metaphor.*
> —Donna Brook

1.

Fire, then
turn the page and

2.

more fire.

3.

I know only a little about it:

fire.

There is something about the color
of the flames that can reveal
what chemicals fuel the fire.

I remember that simple fact.

What color are the flames that rise
off a burning body?

What color were the flames that rose
off my sister's and brother-in-law's bodies?

If they were the same color
does that mean they loved each other?

If they were different
does that mean they were soon to be divorced?

Maybe I should strike a match
to my skin and use the light
to search for the perfect woman
and hold her tightly
against my flames until

4.

she collapses into ash.

5.

If I were, let's say, to come across a burning house
on the way back home from the supermarket

could I change the color of the flames
if I emptied the contents of my shopping bags

onto the blaze? Would the firemen run from hydrant
to hydrant and dodge Golden Delicious apples

while the station house Dalmatian licked
the puddle of Pepsi as the old white man

cursed me for wasting the food
which could feed all of the Third World?

So many questions
and then a Holocaust here, a Holocaust there

6.

a Holocaust everywhere.

7.

Let's say I am a Jew.
I am a Jew
who lost a sister and brother-in-law
in the ovens
during World War II. No, let's say

I am an American
Indian who had heated bayonets
held against his hands
until they blistered
and blossomed open. No, let's say

this all happened to me
because I can't tell the difference
between the size of a metaphor
and the temperature
of the flame. No, let's say

I only believe in two metaphors:
God and God
as the Burning Bush
which uses our questions
like kindling.

8.

On the application for a driver's license, they will ask you this: What do you do, as you are driving down the freeway toward a car aflame with the passenger still trapped inside, when a flicker of insecurity becomes a sudden roar inside you and convinces you there is somebody driving behind you who is much more deserving of saving a life?

9.

a. You drive past the burning car to the next exit, pull into the closest parking lot, and weep violently.

b. You stop the car, open your door, roll to the pavement, and wave your arms wildly, as if you were a small bird too small for flight.

c. You call your mother on your cellular phone and blame her for everything that's gone wrong in your life.

d. You search the radio stations for news of the next solar eclipse.

10.

e. None of the above.

11.

What do you do
when your sister burns
like a bad firework?

She sparks
and sputters
smokes uselessly

and leaves
only a shell
a husk

and the smell
and the smell
and the smell and

12.

it smells exactly like what it is.

13.

There is a grave on the Spokane Indian Reservation
where my sister is buried. I can take you there.

Sonnet: Tattoo Tears

1.

No one will believe this story I'm telling, so it must be true.

2.

It's true: the Indian woman with three tears tattooed under her left eye folded under the weight of her own expectations, after her real tears failed to convince. No disfigurement is small and three tears leave you without choices, without hope or grace. The Indian woman with three tears tattooed under her left eye shot or stabbed her husband and went to prison for murder. In this, I cannot find the slightest measure of music. My hands are empty when I wave Hello, Old Friends to the cancellation of air, to the inversion of possibilities, to the strange animals haunting my dreams.

3.

Strange animals haunt my dreams, animals formed wholly by color, animals chasing me through the gallop of my imagination. But it wasn't Gallup streets I ran through, afraid, and it wasn't Spokane or Seattle, and maybe I wasn't coming nearer to the childhood I forgive most often when I lie in bed all day, refusing to stand and leave the safety of inertia. Most often, the animals have faces, familiar, like each was a cousin by marriage or a promise of destruction, like my ancestors had chosen me for a twentieth century vision.

4.

A twentieth century vision: my sister in San Francisco, early '70s, with a single tear tattooed under her right eye. She is pregnant, her dreams protected by the cardboard box she carries as defense. It's a small kind of medicine. Years later, I search for her in the newsreels, the black-and-white photographs, the glossary of a textbook, look for some definition of her disappearance.

5.

Disappear, child, like a coin in the hands of another reservation magician. Disappear, mother, into a cable television memory, 40 channels of commercials selling the future. What was I thinking, sending cash by mail, $19.95 for a knife that could cut concrete and oranges into halves? Disappear, father, as you close your eyes to sleep in the drive-in theater. What did you tell me? *Movies are worthless. They're just sequels to my life.* Disappear, brother, into the changing river, salmontravelling beneath the uranium mine, all of it measured now by half-lives and miles-between-dams. Disappear, sister, like a paper cut, like a rock thrown through a window, like a Fourth of July firework.

6.

It's the Fourth of July and every Indian looks into the sky. Tears explode from their eyes, louder and brighter than a bottle rocket. Tears lick their cheeks like a Jimi Hendrix solo. Tears fall until they build a new bridge across the Bering Strait. Tears fill up a chipped cup and Big Mom makes it into instant coffee. Tears echo, tears confuse the local weatherman, tears the size of golf balls, tears canned and distributed by the BIA, tears pulled into a hypodermic and mainlined. Tears sprayed onto a slice of white bread and eaten. Tears tattooed under the eyes of Indians who believe everything their mirrors whisper.

7.

Whispering slowly, a pair of panty hose rolled over an ankle sounds like a promise, like a memory fitted tightly over the skin: my sister in the mirror braided her hair into wild ponies, pulled the Goodwill panty hose over her legs and let me rub my cheek against her calves while she waited for some Indian boy or other. What did she used to say? Every weekend can be a powwow if you know what kind of music to play.

8.

What kind of music do you play when drums aren't enough?

9.

The drums aren't loud enough, so the deaf fancydancer stands still, scratching at the tears tattooed under both his eyes. Then, a beer truck roars by outside, shakes the earth like a drum, and the deaf fancydancer two-steps to a horsepowered song.

10.

The jukebox in the bar is horsepowered. The street lights making shadows on the basketball court are horsepowered. Seymour's new drum is diesel, gets great gas mileage but stutters when it climbs hills. On the top of Wellpinit Mountain, I watch for fires, listen to a radio powered by the ghosts of 1,000 horses, shot by the United States Cavalry a century ago, last week, yesterday. My cousins paint red tears under their horses' eyes just before they run at Playfair Race Track. Last I heard, my cousins are still waiting for any of their horses to finish, to emerge from the dust and gallop toward a new beginning.

11.

If I begin this story with the last word, the last spark of flame left from the trailer fire, will you remember everything that came before? If I show you the photograph of my sister just emerged from the sweat house, steam rising from her body like horses, a single tear tattooed under the right eye, can you pretend to miss her? If I tell you her body was found in the ash, the soft edge of the earth, will you believe she attempted escape but couldn't lift her head from the pillow? If I show you the photograph of my sister in her coffin, hair cut short by the undertaker who never knew she called her hair *Wild Ponies*, will you imagine you loved her?

12.

Imagination is the only weapon on the reservation.

13.

The reservation waits for no one. Acre by acre, it roars past history, forgiving and forgetting nothing. There are moments here which can explain your whole life. For instance, the beer can wedged between bars in the cattle guard predicts the next car wreck, but it also sounds like an ocean of betrayal if picked up and held to the ear.

14.

Listen: truth is a strange animal haunting my dreams, my waking. In the reservation Kmart, forty televisions erupt in a 20th century vision: 500 years of bad situation comedies. Measured by the half hour, the Indian woman with three tears tattooed under her left eye disappears into the scenery, into the crowd of another Fourth of July celebration. The soundtrack of her life whispers some kind of music, but it isn't drums because drums are never enough. Can you hear canned laughter roaring out of her horsepowered stereo on the shelf next to her life? What can I tell you about the beginning of her story that would help you imagine how much of the reservation she had tattooed across her skin?

Sister Fire, Brother Smoke

Have I become an accomplished liar,
a man who believes in his inventions?
When I see my sister in every fire,

is it me who sets her in those pyres
and burns her repeatedly? Should I mention
I may have become an accomplished liar,

a man who was absent when his sister died,
but still feeds those flames in the present tense?
When I see my sister in every fire,

am I seeing the shadow that survived her
conflagration? Because of my obsession
have I become an accomplished liar,

who strikes a match, then creates a choir
of burning matches, with the intention
of seeing my sister in every fire?

Is she the whisper of ash floating high
above me? I offer these charred questions.
Have I become an accomplished liar
if I see my sister in every fire?

Grand Entry

The Lover of Maps

She unfolds and folds me
directs me
to an exact place
on the reservation

where nothing is ever written down.
She tells me
our stories are maps
told on a scale

larger than can be held
by our clumsy hands.

How We Learn to Say "Mouth" and "Hand" and "Small of Back"

Body to body
do we create

language?
We are Indian

woman and man
(brown skin

on brown skin)
and don't speak

our tribal languages
so when we touch

I pray, you pray
we pray

that we create
all these words

in the good way
our grandparents did

with our own true tongues.

Marriage

What it comes to is this: bread.

Its creation the product of hunger and imagination.

We forget about it until we see it again on the table.

Tribes have gone to war because of wheat and corn.

When it is all you have to eat, there is never enough.

A sad day, when you first realize the difference between good and
bad bread.

Who first saw its possibilities?

If you feed enough to a bird, its stomach will explode. True or false?

Every culture is measured by its bread.

My mother makes her prodigal bread only when I visit.

It has always been meal for the poor and afterthought for the rich.

I walk by a bakery and realize why smell is the most important sense.

Sunday mornings, we wash it down with coffee, then swallow it dry
as Eucharist that afternoon.

The sacred and the utilitarian share an apartment overlooking the
river.

Grand Entry

She danced
this way, through all
my doors
this nomadic woman

who had danced away
from so much before
then changed her dance
and now calls me

Home. She leaned into me
with all of her stories
and trusted gravity
trusted her sense

of balance, trusted mine.
She leaned into me
with all of her hair
that would not be braided.

She leaned into me
with all of her faith
that would not be traded.
She leaned into me

and asked me to owl dance
and I could not refuse.
She asked me to owl dance
and I remembered how

to dance that way, how
to move my body
with her body, dancing
around a specific fire.

She danced
this way, inside all
my rooms
and changed their shape

this nomadic woman
who is the last curve
completing
the circle of my life.

Drum as Love, Fear, and Prayer

1.

Drums
make everyone feel
like an Indian.

Drums make
everyone feel
like an Indian.

Drums make everyone
feel
like an Indian.

Drums make everyone feel
like an Indian.

Drums make everyone feel like
an Indian.

Drums make everyone feel like an Indian.

2.

I have more faith
in drums

than I have in the people
who play them

I told her
and she said God

is a drum.
I have more faith

in a small drum
because I can carry it

everywhere I go
I told her

and she said God
is the smallest drum.

3.

She said, dance.

It is crazy, I know, how quickly I've learned to love
this dancing, this step-step across the floor

when I'd spent my whole life
without any music. I had promised never to dance

in the white way
if I didn't dance in the Indian way first

but she said dance
refuses color when we are broken down

and embraces color when we are built again
and I believed her

and danced when I heard the drums, the drums,
the drums in her voice.

4.

If love is taken
in its smallest part
will there still be enough
to frighten me? Yes

and no. I mean, if love can be
reduced to a cut bead
then I am not afraid.
But if that cut bead is sewn

into a moccasin or purse, if
that bead is part of a chain
built larger and larger, bead
by bead, then I am afraid.

Here, she said, take this bead
with honor. Then she offered another.

5.

And if I choose to love
this Indian woman
partly because she's Indian

(drum)

and if I choose to love
this Indian woman
mostly because she's Indian

(drum)

then who are you to stop
this love between
an Indian woman and man

(drum)

and who am I, who is she, now
for both of us to make these decisions together?

6.

I have broken
bread with her.

We have prayed together in silent places
where we could hear each other breathe
and in airports and lunchtime restaurants
where nothing wanted to rise above it all

except a few lonely people
with their cigarette smoke.

These prayers have not been easy, how
do we say Indian prayers in English
and which God will answer? Is God red
or white? Do these confused prayers mean

we'll live on another reservation
in that country called Heaven?

7.

Then she tells me Jesus is
still here
because Jesus was
once here

and parts of Jesus are
still floating in the air.
She tells me Jesus' DNA is
part of the collective DNA.

She tells me we are all part
of Jesus, we are all Jesus
in part. She tells me to breathe deep
during all of our storms

because you can sometimes taste Jesus
in a good, hard rain.

8.

And I want to say this (say it)
and I want to whisper (shout)
and I want to shake the doors of the house (church)
and I want to blow a trumpet (play a drum)

and I want to run (dance)
and I want to talk about laughter (pain)
and I want to count up all the losses (magic)
and I want to blow a trumpet (play a drum)

and I want to inventory my fears (joy)
and I want to hide beneath old blankets (grace)
and I want to feast (pray)
and I want to blow a trumpet (play a drum)

and I want
to play a drum.

9.

She danced alone
before she ever knew me

and she'll dance alone
though she loves me

but for now
she dances

with me.
I take her hand.

No.
I take her face

in my hands
and I tell her

how much I believe
in her, in her.

Last Will and Testament

By now, of course, you realize I have lost the house keys again.
Change the dictionary: "bread" now means "book."

I forgot to laugh the last time we made love.
Tell Wovoka we never could dance that long.

What I have accomplished: enough faith to fill my mouth.
Bury a salmon with me.

I still don't know all the words to that song.
Cut your hair and hide the feathers for a year.

What I neglected: rivers.
Leave the television on while you sleep.

I take secrets with me.
Learn how to speak to the Deaf.

Dollar bills are secreted between the pages of every book on my
shelf.
Drive my car until it runs out of gas and leave it where it stops.

I shot an arrow blindly and hit forgiveness.
Keep fresh ice in the freezer.

The birds are not jealous of our thumbs.
Jitterbug; my father can teach you.

With each war, remember I would have opposed it.
Wear my old shirts to work.

Always, somewhere, a boy or girl is bouncing a basketball.
Pray in public places.

Tortilla chips and salsa.
Give my blankets to Indians with short hair.

Not once in my life did I ever want to get out of bed.
Sell our shared home and move into a new place.

I only seriously contemplated killing one person.
Turn the mirrors against the walls.

With all the metaphors in the world at your disposal, mourn.

Tourists

Harmful Jazz

from the *International Herald Tribune*, January 23, 1921

Jazz music is proving too much
for the American Indian,

says Dr. Henry Beets, secretary of the Christian Reformed Church
Missions.
He declares that the jazz and the shimmy are driving the redskin
back to the war dance.

He suggests that the Interior Department stop
Indian maids and youths dancing modern steps,

in order to save their morals and bring them back
to the paths of their fathers.

Owl Dancing with Fred Astaire

During a traditional Native American owl dance, the woman asks the man to dance. He is not supposed to refuse. However, if he does refuse, he must pay the woman whatever she wants and then tell the entire crowd at the powwow exactly why he refused.

1.

I met the Indian woman who asked Fred Astaire to dance.
He had politely refused her offer.

"He was so charming," she said, "even when he rejected me.
But I kept wishing it was an owl dance."

2.

An owl dance is simple: two steps with your left foot forward,
one step with your right foot back, all to the beat of a drum

currently being pounded by six Indian men in baseball hats.
They sing falsetto. Many non-Indians wonder what they are singing

but that is too complicated to explain here. Let's just say
they are singing an owl dance song. It is not necessarily romantic.

I mean, sisters owl dance with brothers
and sons owl dance with their mothers.

Yet, at every powwow, there are beautiful Indian women
who owl dance with beautiful Indian men, all hoping

for love/sex/a brief vacation from loneliness.
I must emphasize, however, that our love lives are not simple.

There are Indian men who have never been asked to owl dance.

Alone in the powwow crowd, these men tap their feet lightly

along with the drums. They sing softly under their breath.
Perhaps they secretly wish they were Fred Astaire.

3.

Fred Astaire is gone now.
He is dead.
He will not be coming back.

However, if you watch his movies
you will notice
that he often smiles.

What was he thinking?
Was he merely pleased with himself
for being Fred Astaire

or was he completely unaware
of the camera and crew?
Was he dancing simply for the love of dancing?

I don't know
and you will never know either.
Only Fred Astaire knew

and he was very good at keeping a secret
or so I am told
by the people who helped keep his secrets.

4.

In my dream, Fred Astaire stumbles (yes, stumbles)
into the powwow and is shocked by the number of Indians

who have survived
the smallpox blankets, U.S. Cavalry, relocation, etc.

He smiles because, well, he is a good man prone to smiling.
(I must emphasize, however, that there are also bad men

who are prone to smiling.) Fred Astaire loves the drums.
He is pleasantly surprised by the quality of the singing.

Such pitch! and timbre! and range! and projection!
Fred Astaire taps his foot. He is wearing a tuxedo.

He is the skinniest white man in the history of the world.
Can you see him? He is not all that handsome

but he looks like a dancer. A great dancer.
In all cultures, women will choose a homely great dancer

over a handsome non-dancer. Fred Astaire is confident.
He waits for the next owl dance to begin.

5.

Ask yourself this: How many times in your life
are you going to be asked to dance? Take that number

and divide it by the sum of the men and/or women
who have expressed deep affection for you.

If that result is X, then Y = heartbreak + X.
And, of course, Y is always equal to Fred Astaire.

Airplane

Up here, where no Indian was ever meant to be
I carry the small and usual things for safety:

generic novel, movie magazine, book of poems
by the latest great poet, bottle of water, and faith

or guilt, depending on the amount of turbulence.
Like everyone else, I believe in God most

when I'm closest to death. How did I become this
Catholic and catholic, wanting to get to Heaven

as painfully and quickly as everyone else?
Maybe I can look out the window and see God

sitting on the wing. Maybe God is in First Class
enjoying a complimentary carafe of red wine.

"If God is on the plane," I told the flight attendant,
"then I am safe." "However," she said, "I don't think

God is on the passenger list." "I just want
to know who has the best chance of saving my life,"

I asked the flight attendant." "The pilot," she said
but it sounded exactly like she said I could survive

any wreck if I said the last word of my latest prayer
at the exactly moment of impact. How did I become this

Indian flying from one anonymous city to another?
They're all anonymous to me. I can't tell

the difference between New York City and Eugene, Oregon.
I woke up one morning in Tulsa and cried

for all the losses, the bleached bones of buffalo
buried out there on the Great Plains, then realized

I was still in San Francisco, waiting for the earthquake
and wanting it to reveal the bones of all the prisoners

drowned and concealed during that long swim
between Alcatraz and the shore. We are all prisoners.

How did I become this poor Indian with his hands folded
into fists, into a tightly wound prayer, as air became ground

and this airplane, my airplane, landed safely
in a light rain? I walked down the stairs, dis-

embarked, and asked the ground crew if they knew
why this Indian was in the exact place

where no Indian was ever meant to be.
"Engineers," they said, but it sounded exactly

like they said there is a thin, unwavering line
between God and the next available flight.

How did I become this crazy
Catholic who steals the navigational flags

and races down the runway, waving at them all, all
those planes trafficking in the dusky sky? I count

one, two, up to seven planes. I count and count.
I wave those flags (I want to light fires) and I wave

those flags (I want to light fires). I want
to bring all of those planes in, bring them all in

even though each plane might contain a madman
because each plane might instead contain the woman

who wants to light a fire. I stand on the runway waving
them all in, with my left arm like this and my right arm

frantic, wanting to know how I became like this,
just like this, wanting to bring everybody back home.

Prayer Animals

Do not try to convince me the United States is anything other than
savannah.
Weeds burst through the sidewalk.
Drought washes the car window, then wipes its face with the same
dirty handkerchief.
Secret meetings.
The newspaper explains about the food chain.

I am the gazelle in braids and powwow jeans.
Sometime before sunset, I scan the horizon, then bend my head to
the stream.
The water is cold and clear.
I have 355 degree vision.
My only question: Will the hunter use the rifle or his teeth?

How to Remodel the Interior of a Catholic Church

The mute carpet must be replaced with mute carpet.
White walls will be scraped clean and painted dark blue.

Half of the original pews should face east while the rest face west.
The parishioners will be performers.

God loves a circus which loves itself.
We shall leave our shoes in the vestibule.

Keep your favorite saint like a coin in your pocket.
Keep your favorite saint like a ringing in your ears.

Hang a small mirror for the Mohawk saint Tekakwitha.
Her smallpox scars disappeared as she died.

The stained glass should be filled with home movies:
Junior imagines a sin, commits the sin, and then is forgiven.

Build nests in the rafters and pray for birds.
Cook simple soups in the kitchen.

Sculpt candles in the shape of beautiful men and women.
Their smoke will still be smoke.

Hope is trying to find a parking space.
Charity is looking for her name tag.

Grace is a child crying in the balcony.
Faith is a woman sitting in a folding chair.

The choir is a jukebox that plays three songs for a quarter.
The priest's pockets are heavy with change.

Capital Punishment

I prepare the last meal
for the Indian man to be executed

but this killer doesn't want much:
baked potato, salad, tall glass of ice water.

(I am not a witness)

It's mostly the dark ones
who are forced to sit in the chair

especially when white people die.
It's true, you can look it up

and this Indian killer pushed
his fist all the way down

a white man's throat, just to win a bet
about the size of his heart.

Those Indians are always gambling.
Still, I season this last meal

with all I have. I don't have much
but I send it down the line

with the handsome guard
who has fallen in love

with the Indian killer.
I don't care who loves whom.

(I am not a witness)

When it's the warden's stew I don't care
if I add too much salt or pepper.

For the boss I just cook.
He can eat what I put in front of him

but for the Indian man to be executed
I cook just right.

The temperature is the thing.
I once heard a story

about a black man who was electrocuted
in that chair and lived to tell about it

before the court decided to sit him back down
an hour later and kill him all over again.

I have an extra sandwich hidden away
in the back of the refrigerator

in case this Indian killer survives
that first slow flip of the switch

and gets hungry while he waits
for the engineers to debate the flaws.

(I am not a witness)

I prepare the last meal for free
just like I signed up for the last war.

I learned how to cook
by lasting longer than any of the others.

Tonight, I'm just the last one left
after the handsome guard takes the meal away.

I turn off the kitchen lights
and sit alone in the dark

because the whole damn prison dims
when the chair is switched on.

You can watch a light bulb flicker
on a night like this

and remember it too clearly
like it was your first kiss

or the first hard kick to your groin.
It's all the same

when I am huddled down here
trying not to look at the clock

look at the clock, no, don't
look at the clock, when all of it stops

making sense: a salad, a potato
a drink of water all taste like heat.

(I am not a witness)

I want you to know I tasted a little
of that last meal before I sent it away.

It's the cook's job, to make sure
and I was sure I ate from the same plate

and ate with the same fork and spoon
that the Indian killer used later

in his cell. Maybe a little piece of me
lodged in his mouth, wedged between

his front teeth, his incisors, his molars
when he chewed down on the bit

and his body arced like modern art
curving organically, smoke rising

from his joints, wispy flames decorating
the crown of his head, the balls of his feet.

(I am not a witness)

I sit here in the dark kitchen
when they do it, meaning

when they kill him, kill
and add another definition of the word

to the dictionary. America fills
its dictionary. We write down kill and everybody

in the audience shouts out exactly how
they spell it, what it means to them

and all of the answers are taken down
by the pollsters and secretaries

who keep track of the small details:
time of death, pulse rate, press release.

I heard a story once about some reporters
at a hanging who wanted the hood removed

from the condemned's head, so they could look
into his eyes and tell their readers

what they saw there. What did they expect?
All of the stories should be simple.

1 death + 1 death = 2 deaths.
But we throw the killers in one grave

and victims in another. We form sides
and have two separate feasts.

(I am a witness)

I prepared the last meal
for the Indian man who was executed

and have learned this: If any of us
stood for days on top of a barren hill

during an electrical storm
then lightning would eventually strike us

and we'd have no idea for which of our sins
we were reduced to headlines and ash.

Tourists

1. *James Dean*

walks everywhere now. He's afraid of fast cars
and has walked this far, arriving
suddenly on the reservation, in search
of the Indian woman of his dreams.
He wants an Indian woman who could pass
for Natalie Wood. He wants an Indian woman
who looks like the Natalie Wood
who was kidnapped by Indians
in John Ford's classic movie, "The Searchers."
James Dean wants to rescue somebody beautiful.
He still wears that red jacket,
you know the one. It's the color of a powwow fire.
James Dean has never seen
a powwow, but he joins right in, dancing
like a crazy man, like a profane clown.
James Dean cannot contain himself.
He dances in the wrong direction. He tears
at his hair. He sings in wild syllables
and does not care. The Indian dancers stop
and stare like James Dean was lightning
or thunder, like he was bad weather.
But he keeps dancing, bumps into a man
and knocks loose an eagle feather.
The feather falls, drums stop.
This is the kind of silence
that frightens white men. James Dean
looks down at the feather
and knows that something has gone wrong.
He looks into the faces of the Indians.
He wants them to finish the song.

2. *Janis Joplin*

sits by the jukebox in the Powwow Tavern,
talking with a few drunk Indians
about redemption. She promises each of them
she can punch in the numbers
for the song that will save their lives.
All she needs is a few quarters, a beer,
and their own true stories. The Indians
are as traditional as drunk Indians can be
and don't believe in autobiography,
so they lie to Janis Joplin about their lives.
One Indian is an astronaut, another killed JFK,
while the third played first base
for the New York Yankees. Janis Joplin knows
the Indians are lying. She's a smart woman
but she listens anyway, plays them each a song,
and sings along off key.

3. *Marilyn Monroe*

drives herself to the reservation. Tired and cold,
she asks the Indian women for help.
Marilyn cannot explain what she needs
but the Indian women notice the needle tracks
on her arms and lead her to the sweat lodge
where every woman, young and old, disrobes
and leaves her clothes behind
when she enters the dark of the lodge.
Marilyn's prayers may or may not be answered here
but they are kept sacred by Indian women.
Cold water is splashed on hot rocks
and steam fills the lodge. There is no place like this.
At first, Marilyn is self-conscious, aware
of her body and face, the tremendous heat, her thirst,
and the brown bodies circled around her.
But the Indian women do not stare. It is dark

inside the lodge. The hot rocks glow red
and the songs begin. Marilyn has never heard
these songs before, but she soon sings along.
Marilyn is not Indian, Marilyn will never be Indian
but the Indian women sing about her courage.
The Indian women sing for her health.
The Indian women sing for Marilyn.
Finally, she is no more naked than anyone else.

How to Write the Great American Indian Novel

All of the Indians must have tragic features: tragic noses, eyes, and arms.
Their hands and fingers must be tragic when they reach for tragic
food.

The hero must be a half-breed, half white and half Indian, preferably
from a horse culture. He should often weep alone. That is mandatory.

If the hero is an Indian woman, she is beautiful. She must be slender
and in love with a white man. But if she loves an Indian man

then he must be a half-breed, preferably from a horse culture.
If the Indian woman loves a white man, then he has to be so white

that we can see the blue veins running through his skin like rivers.
When the Indian woman steps out of her dress, the white man gasps

at the endless beauty of her brown skin. She should be compared to
nature:
brown hills, mountains, fertile valleys, dewy grass, wind, and clear
water.

If she is compared to murky water, however, then she must have a
secret.
Indians always have secrets, which are carefully and slowly revealed.

Yet Indian secrets can be disclosed suddenly, like a storm.
Indian men, of course, are storms. They should destroy the lives

of any white women who choose to love them. All white women
love
Indian men. That is always the case. White women feign disgust

at the savage in blue jeans and T-shirt, but secretly lust after him.
White women dream about half-breed Indian men from horse cultures.

Indian men are horses, smelling wild and gamey. When the Indian man
unbuttons his pants, the white woman should think of topsoil.

There must be one murder, one suicide, one attempted rape.
Alcohol should be consumed. Cars must be driven at high speeds.

Indians must see visions. White people can have the same visions
if they are in love with Indians. If a white person loves an Indian

then the white person is Indian by proximity. White people must
carry
an Indian deep inside themselves. Those interior Indians are half-breed

and obviously from horse cultures. If the interior Indian is male
then he must be a warrior, especially if he is inside a white man.

If the interior Indian is female, then she must be a healer, especially if
she is inside
a white woman. Sometimes there are complications.

An Indian man can be hidden inside a white woman. An Indian
woman
can be hidden inside a white man. In these rare instances,

everybody is a half-breed struggling to learn more about his or her
horse culture.
There must be redemption, of course, and sins must be forgiven.

For this, we need children. A white child and an Indian child, gender
not important, should express deep affection in a childlike way.

In the Great American Indian novel, when it is finally written,
all of the white people will be Indians and all of the Indians will be
ghosts.

The Exaggeration of Despair

I open the door

(this Indian girl writes that her brother tried to hang himself
with a belt just two weeks after her other brother did hang himself

and this Indian man tells us that, back in boarding school,
five priests took him into a back room and raped him repeatedly

and this homeless Indian woman begs for quarters, and when I ask
her about her tribe, she says she's horny and bends over in front of me

and this homeless Indian man is the uncle of an Indian man
who writes for a large metropolitan newspaper, and so now I know
them both

and this Indian child cries when he sits to eat at our table
because he had never known his own family to sit at the same table

and this Indian woman was born to an Indian woman
who sold her for a six-pack and a carton of cigarettes

and this Indian poet shivers beneath the freeway
and begs for enough quarters to buy pencil and paper

and this fancydancer passes out at the powwow
and wakes up naked, with no memory of the evening, all of his
regalia gone)

I open the door

(and this is my sister, who waits years for a dead eagle from the Park
Service, receives it
and stores it with our cousins, who then tell her it has disappeared

though the feathers reappear in the regalia of another cousin
who is dancing for the very first time

and this is my father, whose own father died on Okinawa, shot
by a Japanese soldier who must have looked so much like him

and this is my father, whose mother died of tuberculosis
not long after he was born, and so my father must hear coughing
ghosts

and this is my grandmother who saw, before the white men came,
three ravens with white necks, and knew our God was going to
change)

I open the door
and invite the wind inside.

The Powwow at the End of the World

I am told by many of you that I must forgive and so I shall
after an Indian woman puts her shoulder to the Grand Coulee Dam
and topples it. I am told by many of you that I must forgive
and so I shall after the floodwaters burst each successive dam
downriver from the Grand Coulee. I am told by many of you
that I must forgive and so I shall after the floodwaters find
their way to the mouth of the Columbia River as it enters the Pacific
and causes all of it to rise. I am told by many of you that I must forgive
and so I shall after the first drop of floodwater is swallowed by that
salmon
waiting in the Pacific. I am told by many of you that I must forgive
and so I shall
after that salmon swims upstream, through the mouth of the Columbia
and then past the flooded cities, broken dams and abandoned reactors
of Hanford. I am told by many of you that I must forgive and so I shall
after that salmon swims through the mouth of the Spokane River
as it meets the Columbia, then upstream, until it arrives
in the shallows of a secret bay on the reservation where I wait alone.
I am told by many of you that I must forgive and so I shall after
that salmon leaps into the night air above the water, throws
a lightning bolt at the brush near my feet, and starts the fire
which will lead all of the lost Indians home. I am told
by many of you that I must forgive and so I shall
after we Indians have gathered around the fire with that salmon
who has three stories it must tell before sunrise: one story will teach us
how to pray; another story will make us laugh for hours;
the third story will give us reason to dance. I am told by many
of you that I must forgive and so I shall when I am dancing
with my tribe during the powwow at the end of the world.

What We Notice, What We Miss

Sixty-seven beer bottles hidden beneath the bed
of the departed houseguest who pretended to be sober.

The fence and what is not
the fence.

In 1976, four bald eagles built nests on the power towers above the
dam.
In 1977, they left. In 1994, they returned and built again.

The mirror that hung in the hallway for twenty years
now hangs in the bedroom.

During the powwow, the fancydancers.
Before the powwow, the grandmothers gathering feathers.

The pain of an arm broken in childhood
seconds after we have broken the other arm as an adult.

The ant
carrying God on its shoulders.

To Find Sasquatch

The Sasquatch Poems

Sasquatch: a hairy creature like a human being reported to exist in the northwestern U.S. and western Canada and said to be a primate between 6 and 15 feet tall—called also bigfoot.
—Merriam Webster's Collegiate Dictionary, Tenth Edition

How our hearts are carried off by a hairy monster that may live only in our hearts...
—Robert Michael Pyle, Where Big Foot Walks: Across the Dark Divide

1.

I believe in Sasquatch
just as much as I believe in God
which is not logical
since more people have seen Sasquatch
than have seen God.

2.

We hire priests and politicians
who promise us there are no mysteries
only doors that can be opened easily.

3.

I don't believe doors
are proof of anything
other than doors.

4.

Mystery is a series of large footprints
leading us from the edge of the forest
to the center of the desert.

At the center: an Anasazi pot.

In Hopi, Anasazi means ancient, alien one.
After 1200 A.D. the Anasazi vanished, leaving behind
only the slightest traces of their sudden departure.

Only the Hopi know where they went.

5.

In the year I was born, a Sasquatch chased N
from Benjamin Lake to Turtle Lake.

N was on horseback
and still barely escaped.

N refuses to speak of this even now
and will only smile
when asked about the chase.

6.

Because we are human
we assign human emotions to Sasquatch.
When it chased N from lake to lake
we assume Sasquatch was angry.

How would our hearts change
if we discovered Sasquatch was running
just for the sake of the run, the burn
in the leg muscles and lungs?

7.

We tell these Sasquatch stories
because we are Spokane Indian.

We are Spokane
because our grandparents were Spokane.

Our grandparents told Sasquatch stories.
Our grandparents heard Sasquatch stories

told by their grandparents.
In this way, we come to worship.

8.

By now, the hunters and hobbyists also call them Sasquatch
because they have come to understand a little
of what Indians have always understood.

9.

Headline in the tabloids:
"Bigfoot Baby Found
in Watermelon: Has Elvis's Sneer."

10.

Those who say "Bigfoot"
are those who don't believe.
We must learn to fear metaphor.

11.

We followed the footprints from the source of the stream
to the place where the stream emptied into the river.

We saw its hair snagged on branches ten feet above us.
Its smell was still powerful a full day after it had passed through.

The smell: rotten eggs, sulfur, burned hair, blood, sawdust,
pine sap, bat piss, standing water, split granite, sunlight.

12.

Even now, we like to think science replaced religion
when, in fact, religion became science.

13.

I ran into the house on fire and saved my father and mother.
I ran into the house on fire and saved my sister and brother.
I ran into the house on fire and saved my version of God.
I ran into the house on fire and saved my only effective blanket.
I ran into the house on fire and saved my Adam and Eve.
I ran into the house on fire and saved my porcupine quill.
I ran into the house on fire and saved my cup of ice water.
I ran into the house on fire and saved my metamorphic rock.
I ran into the house on fire and saved my saxophone.
I ran into the house on fire and saved my last will and testament.
I ran into the house on fire and saved my favorite red shirt.
I ran into the house on fire and saved my basketball.
I ran into the house on fire and saved my book about Sasquatch.

14.

After D.B. Cooper hijacked the commercial jet
and parachuted 30,000 feet into the Cascades
where he and his newly acquired money disappeared

we can only assume that he lived
because his death would kill the mystery.
Our only certainty: D.B. Cooper is not Sasquatch.

15.

In order to know what Sasquatch is
we must know what he is not.

16.

Here, I wonder why I speak of Sasquatch as male
when more female Sasquatch have been seen

including the most famous: the Sasquatch woman
who walked across deadfall in the film

shot by Roger Patterson on the Hupa Indian Reservation
in Northern California. We have all seen

her pendulous breasts, prominent brow, large feet
and shadowed eyes as she turns to face the camera,

and the commotion caused when Patterson's horse threw him.
Patterson continued to film as he fell, as he climbed

to his feet, and ran after the Sasquatch. His home movie
has never been discredited, only ignored or dismissed.

17.

The scientists don't want Sasquatch to exist
because her existence would destroy their God.

18.

Roger Patterson was a Yakama Indian
a fact which provides me with a small, secret pleasure.
I have been taught to keep secrets
and to fool you into believing I'll reveal them.

19.

If we sit in John F. Kennedy's limousine on November 22, 1963
and then look back over our shoulder just as the first shot is fired
we will see a shadowy figure in the sixth floor window of the
    Depository.

Moving closer, we can see the rifle, a gold ring, and brown eyes. We can see a bead of sweat fall from forehead to gun stock, soaking into the finely-grained wood. We can see the gray smoke rise.

We do know that Sasquatch did not shoot JFK
but we wonder if the man who pulled the trigger
was hired by the same men who pay the scientists.

20.

On his deathbed, Roger Patterson wished
he had shot the Sasquatch
and proved her existence with a corpse.

21.

Thesis: Indians can only be proven superstitious
if non-Indians are proven to be without superstition.

22.

Do the Sasquatch believe in us?

23.

Do you take the bread and wine
because you believe them to be the body and blood?
I take them, as other Indians do, too
because that colonial superstition is as beautiful
as any of our indigenous superstitions.

24.

Of course, Sasquatch and Indians have known of each other for thousands of years. Certain Indians believed Sasquatch were evil Indians banished from their respective tribes.

Others believed Sasquatch came down from the skies.
Some Indians have sat at lonely campfires and watched
the woods for signs of Sasquatch, their long lost cousin.

25.

A man named Anomaly is over there, in the dark
corner, with his eyes closed, dancing all by himself.

26.

I can give you proof of God: Jim Thorpe, Sac and Fox Indian, won gold medals in the decathlon and pentathlon at the 1912 Stockholm Olympics. He won those medals despite the fact that Indians were not yet recognized as United States citizens.

27.

Sasquatch did not kidnap the Lindbergh baby.
Sasquatch did not bury the empty coffin of Heinrich Müller.
Sasquatch did not kill the prostitutes in Whitechapel.
Sasquatch did not fly with Amelia Earhart.
Sasquatch did not roll the stone away from Jesus' tomb.
Sasquatch did not build the pyramids.
Sasquatch did not create the Ghost Dance.
Sasquatch did not drop the bombs at Hiroshima and Nagasaki.
Sasquatch did not descend from the Missing Link.
Sasquatch did not drag boulders across Easter Island.
Sasquatch did not crash land in Roswell, New Mexico.
Sasquatch did not walk across the Bering Strait.
Sasquatch did not sink Lemuria.
Sasquatch did not write Shakespeare's plays.

28.

I can give you proof of Sasquatch: Indian tribes of the Pacific Northwest carved ape faces into their totem poles long before any Europeans arrived and brought news of such animals. According to the scientists, there are no other primates, aside from human beings, indigenous to North America.

29.

If Sasquatch is the deviation
then what is the common rule?

30.

Late night on the Spokane Indian Reservation
we can hear the shrill cry echo through the pines.

We have recorded the cry and played it for the experts
who cannot tell us which animal made that sound.

31.

Because the Sasquatch use tools, I wonder if they write poems.
Because the Sasquatch steal salmon from nets, I wonder if they have
    justice.
Because the Sasquatch travel alone, I wonder if they love.
Because the Sasquatch travel in families, I wonder if they hate.
Because the Sasquatch smell bad, I wonder if they feel shame.
Because the Sasquatch hide, I wonder if they are afraid.
Because the Sasquatch cry in the night, I wonder if they believe in God.

32.

A large footprint in the damp sand.
A bush burning on the mountain.

33.

When I asked the Indian elder, she said
with a smile, "I don't know if I believe in Sasquatch
but he sure do stink."

Bob's Coney Island

Introduction to Western Civilization

In Spain, on the Mediterranean coast, there is a walled city
which has been inhabited for thousands of years,
though many parts have fallen to ruin, such as the church
which now consists of a wall and an anonymous room.

On the exterior wall of the church, a metal basket extends
toward the sea. I thought it had been used for a game
until Bengt explained that the basket once held the skulls of enemy
soldiers, and served
as a vivid warning against any further attacks on the church.

After the Trial of Hamlet, Chicago, 1994

Did Hamlet mean to kill Polonius? Diane and I sit at a table
with the rich, who have the luxury to discuss such things
over a veal dinner. The vegetables are beautiful! We have just come
from the mock Trial of Hamlet, which is more a fund-raiser
and social gathering, but we must render a verdict. I am here

because I wrote a book which nobody here has read, a book
that Diane reads because she loves me. My book has nothing
to do with Hamlet. My book is filled with reservation Indians.
Maybe my book has everything to do with Hamlet. The millionaire
next to me sets down one of his many forks to shake my hand.

He tells me the poor need the rich more than the rich need the poor.
Abigail Van Buren eats corn at the next table. I read this morning
she has always believed homosexuality is just as genetically determined
as heterosexuality. Finally. Somebody tells the truth. Dear Abby
can have all the corn she wants! I'll pay. She wears a polka-dot dress

and is laughing loudly at something I know is not funny.
Did Hamlet really see his father's ghost? Was there a ghost? Was
Hamlet insane
or merely angry when he thrust his sword through
that curtain and killed Polonius? The millionaire tells me
taxicab drivers, shoe shine men, waiters, and waitresses exist

only because the rich, wearing shiny shoes, often need to be driven
to nice restaurants. A character actor walks by with a glass of wine.
I recognize him because I'm the type of guy who always recognizes
character actors. He knows that I recognize him but I cannot tell
if he wants me to recognize him. Perhaps he is afraid that I am

confusing him with another character actor who is more famous or
less famous.
He might be worried that I will shout his name incorrectly
and loudly, transposing first and last names, randomly inserting
wild syllables that have nothing to do with his name.
Did Hamlet want to have sex with his mother Gertrude? Was Ham-
let mad with jealousy

because Claudius got to have sex with Gertrude? When is a king
more than a king? When is a king less than a king? Diane is beautiful.
She wears red lipstick which contrasts nicely with her brown skin.
We are the only Indians in Chicago! No, we are the only Indians
at the Trial of Hamlet. I hold her hand under the table, holding it

tightly until, of course, we have to separate so we can eat our food.
We need two hands to cut our veal. Yet Diane will not eat veal.
She only eats the beautiful vegetables. I eat the veal and feel guilty.
The millionaire tells me the rich would love a flat tax rate. He talks
about interest rates and capital gains, loss on investments

and trickle-down economics. He thinks he is smarter than me.
He probably is smarter than me, so I tell him insecurely that I wrote
a book.
I know he will never read it. My book has nothing to do
with Polonius. My book is filled with reservation Indians. Maybe it
has everything
to do with Polonius. A Supreme Court Justice

sits at the head table. He decides my life! He eats rapidly. I want to
know how
he feels about treaty rights. I want to know if he feels
guilty about eating the veal. There is no doubt in my mind
the Supreme Court Justice recognizes the beauty of our vegetables.
Was Hamlet a man without logical alternatives? Did he resort

to a mindless, senseless violence? Were his actions those of a tired
and hateful man? Or those of a righteous son? The millionaire introduces his wife,
but she barely acknowledges our presence. Diane is more
gorgeous, though she grew up on reservations and once
sat in a tree for hours, wishing she had lighter skin. Diane wears

a scarf she bought for three dollars. I would ask her to marry me right
now, again, in this city where I asked her to marry me the first time.
But she already agreed to marry me then and has, in fact, married me.
Marriage causes us to do crazy things. She reads my books. I eat veal.
Was Hamlet guilty or not by reason of insanity for the murder of Polonius?

The millionaire tells me how happy he is to meet me. He wishes me
luck. He wants to know what I think of Hamlet's case. He tells me Hamlet,
insane or not, is responsible for what he did. There is always something
beautiful in the world at any given moment. When I was poor I loved
the five-dollar bills I would unexpectedly find in coat pockets. When I feel

tired now, I can love the moon hanging over the old hotels of Chicago.
Diane and I walk out into the cold November air. We hail a taxi.
The driver is friendly, asks for our names, and Diane says, I'm Hamlet,
and this is Hamlet, my husband. The driver wants to know where we're from
and which way we want to go. Home, we say, home.

Inside Dachau

1. *big lies, small lies*

Having lied to our German hosts about our plans
for the day, Diane and I visited Dachau
instead of searching for rare albums in Munich.
Only a dozen visitors walked through the camp
because we were months away from tourist season.
The camp was austere. The museum was simple.

Once there, I had expected to feel simple
emotions: hate, anger, sorrow. That was my plan.
I would write poetry about how the season
of winter found a perfect home in cold Dachau.
I would be a Jewish man who died in the camp.
I would be the ideal metaphor. Munich

would be a short train ride away from hell. Munich
would take the blame. I thought it would all be simple
but there were no easy answers inside the camp.
The poems still took their forms, but my earlier plans
seemed so selfish. What could I say about Dachau
when I had never suffered through any season

inside its walls? Could I imagine a season
of ash and snow, of flames and shallow graves? Munich
is only a short train ride from Dachau.
If you can speak some German, it is a simple
journey which requires coins and no other plans
for the day. We lied about visiting the camp

to our German hosts, who always spoke of the camp
as truthfully as they spoke about the seasons.
Dachau is still Dachau. Our hosts have made no plans
to believe otherwise. As we drove through Munich
our hosts pointed out former Nazi homes, simply
and quickly. "We are truly ashamed of Dachau,"

Mikael said, "but what about all the Dachaus
in the United States? What about the death camps
in your country?" Yes, Mikael and Veronika, you ask simple
questions which are ignored, season after season.
Mikael and Veronika, I'm sorry we lied about Munich
and Dachau. I'm sorry we lied about our plans.

Inside Dachau, you might believe winter will never end. You might
lose faith in the change of seasons
because some of the men who built the camps still live in Argentina,
in Washington, in Munich.
They live simple lives. They share bread with sons and daughters
who have come to understand the master plan.

2. *history as home movie*

It begins and ends with ash, though we insist
on ignoring the shared fires in our past.
We attempt to erase our names from the list
that begins and ends with ash.

We ignore the war until we are the last
standing, until we are the last to persist
in denial, as we are shipped off to camps

where we all are stripped, and our dark bodies lit
by the cruel light of those antique Jew-skinned lamps.
Decades after Dachau fell, we stand in mist
that begins and ends with ash.

3. *commonly asked questions*

Why are we here? What have we come to see?
What do we need to find behind the doors?
Are we searching for an apology

from the ghosts of unrepentant Nazis?
We pay the entrance fee at the front door.
Why are we here? What have we come to see?

The actors have moved on to the next scene
and set: furnace, shovel, and soot-stained door.
Are we searching for an apology

from all the Germans who refused to see
the ash falling in front of their locked doors?
Why are we here? What have we come to see

that cannot be seen in other countries?
Every country hides behind a white door.
Are we searching for an apology

from the patient men who've hidden the keys?
Listen: a door is a door is a door.
Why are we here? What have we come to see?
Are we searching for an apology?

4. *the american indian holocaust museum*

What do we indigenous people want from our country?
We stand over mass graves. Our collective grief makes us numb.
We are waiting for the construction of our museum.

We too could stack the shoes of our dead and fill a city
to its thirteenth floor. What did you expect us to become?
What do we indigenous people want from our country?

We are waiting for the construction of our museum.

We are the great-grandchildren of Sand Creek and Wounded Knee.
We are the veterans of the Indian wars. We are the sons
and daughters of the walking dead. We have lost everyone.
What do we indigenous people want from our country?
We stand over mass graves. Our collective grief makes us numb.
We are waiting for the construction of our museum.

5. *songs from those who love the flames*

We start the fires
on the church spire:
ash, ash.
We build tall pyres
from children's choirs:
ash, ash.
We watch flames gyre
and burn the liars:
ash, ash.

We watch flames gyre
from children's choirs:
ash, ash.
We start the fires
and burn the liars:
ash, ash.
We build tall pyres
on the church spire:
ash, ash.

We build tall pyres
and burn the liars:
ash, ash.
We watch flames gyre
on the church spire:

ash, ash.
We start the fires
from children's choirs:
ash, ash.

6. *after we are free*

If I were Jewish, how would I mourn the dead?
I am Spokane. I wake.

If I were Jewish, how would I remember the past?
I am Spokane. I page through the history books.

If I were Jewish, how would I find the joy to dance?
I am Spokane. I drop a quarter into the jukebox.

If I were Jewish, how would I find time to sing?
I am Spokane. I sit at the drum with all of my cousins.

If I were Jewish, how would I fall in love?
I am Spokane. I listen to an Indian woman whispering.

If I were Jewish, how would I feel about ash?
I am Spokane. I offer tobacco.

If I were Jewish, how would I tell the stories?
I am Spokane. I rest my hands on the podium.

If I were Jewish, how would I sleep at night?
I am Spokane. I keep the television playing until dawn.

If I were Jewish, how would I find my way home?
I am Spokane. I step into the river and close my eyes.

7. *below freezing*

Dachau was so cold I could see my breath
so I was thankful for my overcoat.
I have nothing new to say about death.

Each building sat at right angles to the rest.
Around each corner, I expected ghosts.
Dachau was so cold I could see my breath.

Everything was clean, history compressed
into shoes, photographs, private notes.
I have nothing new to say about death.

I wanted to weep. I wanted to rest
my weary head as the ash mixed with snow.
Dachau was so cold I could see my breath.

I am not a Jew. I was just a guest
in that theater which will never close.
I have nothing new to say about death.

I wonder which people will light fires next
and which people will soon be turned to smoke.
Dachau was so cold I could see my breath.
I have nothing new to say about death.

Reading Harvey Shapiro's Poetry While Standing in Line to See Tom Hanks in *Apollo 13*

I am afraid of space, the lack of gravity, the immeasurable cold.
I am afraid of the distance between Tom Hanks and Harvey Shapiro.

Harvey Shapiro lives in Brooklyn Heights.
He sits by his window and listens to the neighbors.

A lonely car drives by his brownstone at three in the morning.
Why is it lonely? It is not loved.

More than anything, I am afraid of not being loved.
I want to stand under Harvey's window

and wail like a dumb cat.
Throw a shoe at me, Harvey, throw a shoe!

Jesus, I grew up on a reservation
and I wonder...

but there is no time to wonder.
This is America. We check our hats at the door
and jump into the heated debate.

The debate: Should we be spending billions
to send men and women into space
when there are people starving in Brooklyn Heights?

In Brooklyn Heights!

Norman Mailer lives in Brooklyn Heights
and thinks he knows the answer
so he is writing yet another epic novel.
Somebody needs to teach Norman about the haiku.

Harvey Shapiro, what do you say?
Harvey strokes his beard. Harvey smiles.

A strong wind could blow a star-shaped hole right through both of us.

Things (for an Indian) to Do in New York (City)

1.

Walk down the Avenue of the Americas
though it's actually Sixth Avenue
and I mean walk right down the middle
of the Avenue of the Americas

and tell all of the cab drivers I love them
or walk down the middle of Wyckoff Street
in Brooklyn at three in the morning
waving my arms like a crazy man

because some New Yorker once told me
it will scare all of the muggers away
but I think it means those muggers
will just end up mugging an Indian

acting like a crazy man
but maybe I could make them laugh
and they'd leave me enough money
for another cannoli, cannoli, cannoli

or I might convince myself that I look more
like a mugger than one who is to be mugged
because I have dark skin, long hair
and those dark-skinned, long-haired muggers
will all nod their heads at me

whenever I walk by, brother to brother
but wait, everybody is a mugger
and that white man in a wool suit
just lifted my wallet
and disappeared down the Avenue

of the Americas, which, as we all know
by now, is actually Sixth Avenue
and lucky me, he took my throw-down
wallet, which only held a twenty
and a sepia photograph of Mister X.

2.

Read Ted Berrigan's sonnets
and wonder how we are all alike
but still have absolutely nothing

in common. I stop bearded men
and beautiful women in the streets
and they're all poets. Everybody

is bearded and beautiful. Everybody
is a poet. I roll a drunk over
in a doorway and he quotes

Robert Frost. My God, he's home-
less and formalist. How much money
should I drop into his tin cup?

3.

The whole world does not belong
in any one place, but here we are

all of us gathered in Times Square
with guns drawn and teeth bared.

I want to find somebody to kill
because of their skin color. No.

I want to kill a busload of children

because of their parents' religion

and I want to build a hate machine
in the middle of Times Square

and call it a piano. I want
to start a circus in Manhattan

and call it a church. I want to hail
a mounted policeman and call him God.

4.

What time is it? I stop
a passerby in this cruel city
and ask her. It's 12:02 p.m.

she tells me and keeps
walking. She actually gave me
the correct time. Oh, the kindness

and I stop watch-wearer
after watch-wearer, asking
for the time and they all give it to me.

I could live here
forever. No, that's not true
at all. I'm lying

because it's nearly 1:34 p.m.
and I have three hours to kill
before the matinee show.

5.

There is nothing as sad as a bad guitar player
in the hotel room next door at some insane hour

moving his clumsy fingers from chord to chord
until you think, in those long pauses between
B flat and F, that he must be an Indian
adopted as a young child by a white family, and now
confused and desperate, has come to New York City
to become a rock star, but hocks his guitar
eventually for a bus ticket back home
to his white parents, who love him so much
they don't say a word about his new braids
and they all travel to a powwow together
slightly embarrassed to find their feet tapping
along in an imperfect rhythm with the drums.

6.

I was looking for a happy ending
but instead found a refrigerator

abandoned on East Fifth Street.
Then I found a couch

a dining table with three chairs
and a microwave oven. I found

a lamp, a coffee table, and a television.
I found a perfect pair of shoes.

7.

I think how when I left the reservation
my entire world, which had been brown, became white
but this is New York City and everybody is brown
but this is America, too, and everybody is still
white, but then again, I know America is not white
exactly, but it is white inexactly, without
color, needing this or that blood to stain its hands.

8.

On some of these days
there would be too much to do
so I don't even leave
the Brooklyn brownstone

and I'm frightened
because I'm an Indian
who knows the difference
between Monet and Manet

so I just watch TV
because I am an American
Indian and the walk to the subway
can break both of my hearts.

9.

On TV, more soccer riots in Europe.
There would be riots in American stadiums
during our particular games
if the people who had reason to riot
could pay the price for admission.

10.

But, America, I think how
your men will always find
a more effective way to kill.

No Indian would have ever invented
an automatic bow and arrow
but I love you still

in the way I have been taught
to love you:
with fear.

11.

So how is it possible
that I could fall in love
with every waitress
and waiter in Manhattan?

Stop. I'm not in love
with any of them.
It must be the food.
But they are gorgeous

though horrible at their jobs
so when they drop
the plates and cups
it still sounds like music.

12.

Then I think to thank all of you
for Emily Dickinson and Walt Whitman

for the automobile and Orson Welles
for fluoride in the drinking water.

13.

Suddenly, there's another Indian on the subway
sitting right beside me, surprise, there's an Indian
on the subway, F Train from Brooklyn
to Manhattan, on a Monday afternoon, surprise
there is another Indian, I mean, another American

Indian sitting on the subway seat next to me—
really, in the seat right beside me, our legs touch
and I am convinced that she's Indian, Native
American, Aboriginal, beneath her clothes
and she's Indian in her clothes, and her clothes are Indian
because she's wearing them. There's an Indian
on the F Train all the way from Brooklyn
to Manhattan. She's my wife, and she loves me,
she loves me, she loves me.

Going to the Movies with Geronimo's Wife

If you go to the movies with Geronimo's wife
remember to sing her an honor song.

She misses the desert.
She carries blue stones in her pocket.

If you go to the movies with Geronimo's wife
remember to give her your favorite blanket.

She sits by the fire.
She wears blue stones on her hands.

If you go to the movies with Geronimo's wife
remember that her children are ghosts.

She dances.
She weaves blue stones through her hair.

If you go to the movies with Geronimo's wife
remember that her husband is gone.

She sleeps alone.
She lies down on blue stones.

If you go to the movies with Geronimo's wife
remember that she is your sister.

She keeps your secrets.
She hides blue stones behind her eyes.

If you go to the movies with Geronimo's wife
remember to share your last piece of bread.

She knows hunger.
She feeds you blue stones.

If you go to the movies with Geronimo's wife
remember to tell her a good story.

She listens.
She hears blue stones singing.

If you go to the movies with Geronimo's wife
remember that she has a name.

She owns many names.
She whispers them only to blue stones.

The Museum of Tolerance

has opened its doors
and, as agreed, we forgive all sins.

We check our coats
and regretfully remember
the twentieth century: War, war, war, war
followed closely by manned space flight.

I have the sudden urge to telephone old girlfriends and apologize!

This is the Museum of Tolerance: one room
with its one exhibit placed on a white satin pillow
which rests comfortably on an antique maple chair.

The exhibit: a small, red stone.

What does it mean? The debate begins simply enough
but adjectives and adverbs soon fill the room.

A man says, "If I am going to love somebody
then she must love me first."

Flashbulbs, the whir of advancing film.

The Museum of Tolerance, thank God, is open all night
but nobody can agree on the price of admission.

Airplane, Airport, Airline, Air in the Bottom of the Ninth Inning

1.

Over Albuquerque, we look down to see all
of those complicated streets
which will forever cause pizza deliverymen of the future to lose their
way,
but which are empty now, where no houses have been built yet, but
where those houses will soon be developed.

(Whole neighborhoods will rise in-
organically from the desert floor.)

Then, here and there, original in its frame, a solitary house,
once loosely connected to the city
now surrounded by those streets and ghosts and ghosts of houses and
streets-to-be.
There must be an old man waiting all alone in one of those solitary
houses

(Is he white, Indian, Mexican
or does it matter? It matters, doesn't it?)

knowing that, soon, very soon, somebody else's idea
of the West will come knocking loudly at his front door.

2.

We both saw Yanni, New Age musician and hero
of late night television commercials, in the Denver
Airport at the same time, although Diane said his name
aloud before I could actually remember his name
and it was exciting for a moment, our brush with
celebrity, but then I remembered Yanni is

not all that famous, this is just America, and Diane
and I kept our distance, more intent on making our next
connection, but I wonder how we would have reacted if
Chuck Berry had come strolling into our lives, oh, turn
down the goddamn flutes and harps, pound those keyboards
until Beethoven rolls over, rolls over, give Chuck his
guitar and we'd be dancing, dancing up and down
the escalators, we'd be that much more in love.

3.

Southwest Airlines is coming to Spokane, they've arrived in Spokane
with their discount flights
to almost anywhere. Well, that's not true. They only fly to those cities
where the planes can land,
unload, and depart in thirty minutes or so. Oh, cheap flights, cheap
flights. I can get on a plane here
in the Spokane Airport and end up in Oakland, Los Angeles, on the
Pine Ridge Indian Reservation
in South Dakota, but let's not get carried away. I can barely breathe. I
want to find somebody to love
who will fly in the seat beside me and hold my hand, maybe take up
half of the two-for-one fare.
But wait, I'm already in love and I'm rich, rich, rich, so who cares
about cheap flights. I'm an Indian
with money and that makes me dangerous. The flight attendants are
nervous because they know I don't belong
on a Southwest flight. They wanted to leave me waiting forever in
the airport, but they couldn't do it
because I walked perfectly through the metal detector, because I
bought my ticket with cash,
because this is a democracy. Oh, I love these flight attendants. They
are white Americans
in company polo shirts and matching shorts. They have skinny,
tanned legs and I watch their calf muscles
when they walk up and down the aisles. I am not in love with them,

I lied, but I am in love with Indians,
and I want to buy tickets for every Indian on my reservation, and we
can all choose between orange juice
and water, between the 6 a.m. flight and the noon flight, because the
time of departure makes
all the difference, because I want to be the very first passenger to
read the airline magazine.

4.

Mitch Williams, fastball pitcher for the Philadelphia Phillies, gave up the 1993 World Series winning home run in the bottom of the ninth inning to Joe Carter, outfielder for the Toronto Blue Jays.

This is not a metaphor.

Mitch Williams threw the one pitch by which his whole life will be forever measured, and Joe Carter could strike out in every plate appearance he makes during the rest of his life and everybody would still remember his World Series home run.

This is not a metaphor.

I think of those baseball players tonight as I crawl into bed with my wife. The sheets are cold and it's snowing outside, which means that the sheets are cold and it's snowing outside. I know there is somebody playing baseball in this city right now, despite the cold and snow, and I want to thank them for their passion.

Baseball is not a metaphor.

Let's say I pull my wife closer to me under the covers. No. Let's say she pulls me closer under the covers. I might be thinking of Mitch Williams and Joe Carter. She might be thinking of Mitch Williams and Joe Carter, too. Who can explain what we think about when we are making love? I can be suddenly distracted by news of the world. The radio is turned off because she cannot concentrate if the radio plays a song she knows.

She listens too closely to the lyrics.

Afterwards in the dark, I try not to fall asleep because she once read that a man only feels sleepy immediately following orgasm. If he can stay awake for a few minutes, then he can stay awake forever. I am awake. I look through the dark, try to find her features, touch her face, her back, her arm. Although I cannot see for sure, I know her eyes are open. She touches my face. I fall asleep. I dream about Mitch Williams and Joe Carter.

Bob's Coney Island

Let's begin with this: America.
I want it all back
now, acre by acre, tonight. I want
some Indian to finally learn
to dance the Ghost Dance right
so that all of the salmon and buffalo return
and the white men are sent back home
to wake up in their favorite European cities.

I am not cruel.

Still, I hesitate
when Bob walks us around his Coney Island:
  the Cyclone still running
  the skeleton of the Thunderbolt
  the Freak Show just a wall of photographs
  the Parachute Drop
which has not been used in 30 years
but still looks like we could
tie a few ropes to the top (Why the hell not?) and drop
quickly down, spinning, unraveling
watching Bob's Coney Island rise
from the ashes of the sad, old carnival
that has taken its place now, this carnival
that is so sad because, like Diane says

all carnivals are sad.

We drop to the ground, our knees buckle slightly
at impact. We turn to look at each other
with the kind of love and wonder
that only fear and the release of fear can create.
We climb to the top and parachute down

again and again, because there is an ocean
a few feet away, because Manhattan is just a moment
down the horizon, because there was a 13-year-old boy
who believed that Coney Island belonged to him
though we know that all we see
doesn't really belong to anyone

but I'll let Bob have a conditional lease
because I know finally
somebody will take care of this place
even if just in memory.

Produced at The Print Center., Inc., 225 Varick St., New York, NY 10014, a non-profit facility for literary and arts-related publications. (212) 206-8465